THE HEART IS A LITTLE

TO THE LEFT

THE
HEART
IS A LITTLE
TO THE
LEFT

Essays on Public Morality

℃

William Sloane Coffin

Dartmouth College

PUBLISHED BY UNIVERSITY PRESS OF NEW ENGLAND

HANOVER AND LONDON

Dartmouth College

Published by University Press of New England, Hanover, NH 03755

© 1999 by William Sloane Coffin

Printed in the United States of America

5 4 3 2 1

CIP data appear at the end of the book

The author gratefully acknowledges permission to reproduce "A Mirrored Gallery" from *The Collected Poems: 1931-1987* by Czeslaw Milosz. Translated by Renata Gorczynski and Robert Hass. Copyright © 1988 by Czeslaw Milosz Royalties, Inc. Reprinted by permission of The Ecco Press.

To my grandsons, Alex and Julian

Contents

Preface

Everyone is in danger of succumbing to what de Toc-queville called "paltriness of aim." All too frequently we become as ants on a log, arguing with each other as the log approaches the waterfall.

Today the currents of history are indeed churning into rapids and waterfalls. If we are to be equal to the times we live in and to the greater problems the future will bring, we had better learn to scorn trifles and strive to be far more imaginative and more generous in spirit. Above all, I believe we need to claim the kinship of all people, to recover the prophetic insight that we belong one to another, every one of us from the pope to the loneliest wino on the planet. From a religious perspective, that's the way God made us. From a Christian perspective, Christ died to keep us that way, which means that our sin is only and always that we put asunder what God has joined together.

I also believe Pope Pius VI was absolutely correct in saying, "If you want peace, work for justice." The world is fast becoming a global village. Naturally enough, the powerful and wealthy tend to see themselves as the village elders. Their primary preoccupation, however, is with order rather than justice, and history has shown that concern for disorder over injustice generally produces more of both.

The same dangerous possibility confronts Americans when hard-riding, right-leaning Republicans craft tax breaks for billionaires while claiming that the sky would fall were the minimum wage raised to anything approaching a living wage. At the same time, I think we can perceive everywhere in the world a halting yet steady progress toward greater human rights.

The following speeches and sermons on matters of public concern were delivered, for the most part, to university audiences consisting of religious believers and nonbelievers (Ripon, Dartmouth, Mount Holyoke, and Smith colleges and Lawrence University), as well as Riverside Church in New York City and the Presbyterian Church in Saratoga Springs, New York. My primary hope in publishing them is that they might provoke further discussion; for if, without defensiveness, we can face and discuss rather than avoid or deny controversial issues, good results are all but inevitable.

March 1999   W.S.C.

THE HEART IS A LITTLE

TO THE LEFT

THE SPIRITUAL
AND THE SECULAR: CAN
THEY MEET?

℃

MY ORIGINAL INTENT was to give a speech roughly ri-
valing in length one of Fidel Castro's. But I was told
that would never do; what was expected was an abundance of wisdom in an economy of words. So, to save
time, I'm going to assume that you, Mr. President,[1] and
all here present, know how honored and grateful I am
to be part of what Anglicans call your "enthronement."
In no more than twenty minutes, let's see now if, without offense to either, we can't bring the spiritual and the
secular into closer harmony in fine colleges like Ripon.

As all of you know, most churches and colleges in this
country were once wed. Then most got divorced, the
colleges pleading mental cruelty. But apart, they're not

1. Paul B. Ranslow was inaugurated as president of Ripon College, Ripon,
Wisconsin, September 29, 1996.

I

faring well. The religious communities—Jews, Moslems, Christians—need the intellectual rigor of the academic community, while many college professors and students are perishing alive for want of spiritual nourishment.

Spirituality means to me living the ordinary life extraordinarily well. But I know it can mean other things, many of them questionable. When, for example, in Louisiana a few years ago, David Duke won not only 55 percent of the White vote but also 69 percent of White born-again Protestants, you have to ask, "What kind of spirituality is that? Can you be a holy racist? Isn't justice the ethical test of any form of spirituality?"

But "abusus non tollit usum," as Roman Catholics used to say in the old Latin-speaking days, "misuse does not negate right use"; and I would like to suggest three spiritual benefits that I believe can render more fruitful the life of the mind.

Let me start by reading, in translation, a poem of Czeslaw Milosz, a Pole long exiled who, more years than some of us here have lived, has rowed into the teeth of one gale after another. Yet he writes:

> Pure beauty, benediction: you are all I gathered
> From a life that was bitter and confused,

In which I learned about evil, my own and not my own.
Wonder kept dazzling me, and I recall only wonder,
The risings of the sun in boundless foliage,
Flowers opening after the night, universe of grasses,
A blue outline of the mountains and a shout of hosanna.
How many times I thought: is this the truth of the Earth?
How can laments and curses be turned into hymns?
Why do I pretend when I know so much?
But the lips praised on their own, the feet on their own were
    running,
The heart was beating strongly, and the tongue proclaimed
    adoration.[2]

"Wonder kept dazzling me." Aristotle too thought we should approach life with wonder, failing only to add that we should end it in the same way.

But too many of his descendants approach life with doubt—"Dubito, ergo sum." Not that doubts are unimportant. All of us tend to hold certainty dearer than truth. We want to learn only what we already know; we want to become only what we already are. Too frequently even scholarly minds are biased by what they already know, warped by habits of thought; and doubts, Lord knows, are important for the development of reli-

2. Czeslaw Milosz, "A Mirrored Gallery," *The Collected Poems: 1931–1987*, trans. Renata Gorczymski (Ecco Press, 1988).

gious faith if, with St. Augustine, you "believe in thinking and wish to think in believing."

But if doubts are important, wonder is all-important.
None of us scoffs at the stars, nor do we sneer at sun-
sets. Yet we depreciate so much else, it seems almost inevitable that, as civilization advances, the sense of wonder declines. We forget that both the tree of life and the
tree of knowledge are deeply rooted in the soil of mystery. The most incomprehensible fact is the fact that we
comprehend at all.

And wonder is not reserved for beauty alone; it has
an ethical dimension, it leads to reverence. And what an
irony it is that just as technology frees us to be fully human—not mere survivors of the earth's rigors, but
thinking, feeling human beings—how ironic, and sav-
agely so, that soon we may lose the whole planet because we have lost our sense of wonder. For finally, only
reverence can restrain violence, violence against nature,
violence against one another.

We say a little education is dangerous. But a lot is
lethal; it takes a Ph.D. to build a nuclear weapon. So for
the sake of the planet as for that of honest scholarship,
wonder/reverence and knowledge must find each other,
re-wed, and stay married.

Wouldn't it be marvelous if, upon retirement, professors could say, "Wonder kept dazzling me and I recall only wonder" for "the larger the island of knowledge, the longer the shoreline of wonder" (Huston Smith).

Moving on. A distinguished Harvard professor wrote: "In order to fight poverty we feed the horses, hoping the sparrows will eventually benefit."

When the powerful do as they will and the poor suffer as they must, it's easy to become bitter. In fact, it's comforting to be bitter. But it's not creative, bitterness being such a diminishing emotion. Far more productive is anger, which, if focused, is spiritual nourishment for those perishing alive for want of it.

Too many in the academic world are not easily enough disturbed. Some even call to mind Francis Macomber, of whom Hemingway wrote: "He had a great tolerance about him, which would have been a virtue had it not been so insidious."

By and large, the academic world is tolerant. But it tends toward passivity, and tolerance and passivity are a deadly combination. Together they allow us to tolerate the intolerable, to ignore the power of anger in works of love; for if you lessen your anger at the structures of power you lower your love for the victims of power.

I stress anger because the country as a whole is despiritualized by moral lassitude. Having gotten used to genocidal weapons, are we now going to get used to starving children? Instead of their callous advisors, our presidential candidates should be heeding King Lear:

> Take physic, pomp,
> Expose thyself to feel what wretches feel.

Colleges, like churches, tend to be long on charity, short on justice. Karl Marx saw the difference when, addressing a group of church people, he said: "You Christians have a vested interest in unjust structures which produce victims to whom you then can pour out your hearts in charity."

Of course, the insight was biblical before it was Marxist. Those indignant biblical prophets sought less to alleviate the effects of poverty than to eliminate the causes of it. I like Saint Augustine's observation: "Hope has two beautiful daughters. Their names are anger and courage; anger at the way things are, and courage to see that they do not remain the way they are."

But in all this talk of anger, there is a caveat to be entered. We have to hate evil, else we're sentimental. But if we hate evil more than we love the good, we become good haters, and of those the world already has too many. However deep, our anger must always and only measure our love.

And that brings me to the third and most important spiritual benefit. Professors and students are rightly suspicious of religious people. But once again, "misuse does not negate right use." You remember how, with unconscious eloquence, Saint Paul wrote: "Now abide faith, hope, love, these three; and the greatest of these is love."[3] And his very next sentence reads, "Make love your aim."

Too many religious people make faith their aim. They think "the greatest of these" is faith, and faith is defined as all but infallible doctrine. These are the dogmatic, divisive Christians, more concerned with freezing the doctrine than warming the heart.

If faith can be exclusive, love can only be inclusive.

"Make love your aim." Shouldn't that be an added intentional aim of every college and university? Recognizing that the acquisition of knowledge is second to its use, shouldn't colleges want to encourage students not to make money but to make a difference, not to be "successful" but to be valuable, to seek the common good, not private gain?

And how better to encourage them to do so than by concrete hands-on experiences—values are more caught than taught—followed by rigorous classroom analysis

3. See 1 Corinthians 13:13.

to raise to a conscious level the knowledge inherent in the experiences?

Those who live in safety rarely understand lives steeped in misery. I believe every First World student should have a Third World experience, here in this country or abroad.

In my old age I've become a professor, so maybe I'm free, as I wasn't before, to suggest that "cogito, ergo sum"—I think, therefore I am—is a bit of surpassing nonsense. "Amo, ergo sum"—I love, therefore I am—is so much truer, for "though I have all faith so as to move mountains" and "understand all mysteries and all knowledge but have not love, it profits me nothing."[4]

I believe that. I believe it is better not to live than not to love.

Wonder, anger, love. With that trinity of spiritual benefits you can live an ordinary life extraordinarily well. With that trinity the spiritual and the secular can not only come into closer harmony, they can become dynamically integrated! Wonder, anger, love—maybe they're all that's needed to redeem the academic enterprise. Mr. President, Ripon College, show us the way!

4. See 1 Corinthians 13:2.

THE POLITICS OF
COMPASSION

℃

ONE OF THE GREAT church people in this hemisphere is Archbishop Helda Camara of Recife, Brazil. I once heard him say, with a broad smile and in a heavy accent: "Right hand, left hand—both belong to ze same body but ze heart is a little to ze left."

I tell you this story because I too believe that "ze heart is a little to ze left." You don't have to give socialist answers, but you do have to press socialist questions. These are the ones that point toward greater social justice.

Tonight I want to talk as a convinced Christian, the better to refute the answers of my fellow Christians "a little to ze right."

In religious faith, simplicity comes in at least two distinct forms. One lies on the near side of complexity. Those of us who embrace this kind of simple faith dislike, in fact are frightened by, complexity. We hold certainty dearer than truth. We prefer obedience to discernment. Too many of us bear out Charles Darwin's contention that ignorance more frequently begets confidence than does knowledge. And apparently such religious folk were as abundant in Jesus' time as they clearly are in ours. Also, in Jesus' time, as in ours, conventional religious wisdom stressed correct belief and right behavior.

Then there is the religious simplicity that lies on the far side of complexity. That's where, I believe, we must look for Jesus and his message. I believe that when all's said and done, when every subtle thing has been dissected and analyzed every which way, Jesus' message remains incredibly simple, unbelievably beautiful, and as easy to translate into action as for a camel to pass through the eye of a needle.

Nowhere is this simple message more clearly stated than in the parable of the Good Samaritan (found in the tenth chapter of Luke). I hardly need remind you that the two men who passed by on the other side, the priest and the Levite, were considered the most religious persons in the Israelite community, dedicated as they were to the preservation of the faith through full-time religious service. But the third man—the one

who showed mercy, who had compassion, who proved
neighbor to the bleeding man on the side of the road—
this Samaritan was only part Jew and believed only part
of the Jewish Scripture. To Jews, Samaritans were
heretics; Samaria was a dangerous place. Yet it was the
heretic, the enemy, the man of the wrong faith who did
the right thing while the two men of the right faith
flunked.

The same simple, subversive message comes through
in Jesus' other well-known parable. Of course we tend
to identify with the older brother of the prodigal son
because, like him, we want the irresponsible kid to get
what he deserves. But the prodigal love of the father insists that the son get not what he deserves but what he
needs—forgiveness, a fresh start, which is exactly what
—thank God—God gives all of us. We can't be relieved
of the consequences of our sin, but we can be relieved of
the consequences of being sinners; for there is more
mercy in God than sin in us. Wrong behavior is not the
last word.

The culture of his time prevented Saint Paul from
seeing many things, but the simplicity, beauty, and diffi-
culty of Jesus' message was not one of them. He ends 1
Corinthians 13 with "And now abide faith, hope, love,
these three. And the greatest of these is *love*." And he be-

gins the next, the fourteenth chapter: "Make love your aim."

Make love your aim, not biblical inerrancy, nor purity, nor obedience to holiness codes. Make love your aim, for "Though I speak with the tongues . . . of angels"—musicians, poets, preachers, you are being addressed; "and though I understand all mysteries and have all knowledge"—professors, your turn; "and though I give all my goods to feed the poor"—radicals take note; "and though I give my body to be burned"—the very stuff of heroism; "but have not love, it profiteth me nothing."[1] I doubt if in any other scriptures of the world there is a more radical statement of ethics: if we fail in love, we fail in all things else.

So Socrates was mistaken: it's not the unexamined life that is not worth living; it's the uncommitted life. There is no smaller package in the world than that of a person all wrapped up in himself. Love is our business; if we can't love, we're out of business. And all this Christians learn primarily through the words and deeds of that "love divine all loves excelling, joy of heaven to earth come down."

In short, love is the core value of Christian life. And the better to understand what we're saying, let's briefly

1. See 1 Corinthians 13:1–3.

review four major ethical stages in history. Most people shudder when they hear "an eye for an eye" and "a tooth for a tooth." But far from commanding revenge, the law insists that a person must never take more than *one* eye for an eye, never more than *one* tooth for a tooth. Found in the Book of Exodus, this law became necessary to guard against the normal way people had of doing business, namely, unlimited retaliation: "Kill my cat and I'll kill yours, your dog, your mule, and you, too."[2]

The father/mother of unlimited retaliation is, of course, the notion that might makes right, an uncivilized concept if ever there was one and one that to this day governs the actions of many so-called civilized nations. So limited retaliation is certainly an improvement over unlimited retaliation: "Get even but no more." Limited retaliation is what most people have in mind when they speak of criminal justice—"You did the crime, you do the time." Limited retaliation is also the justification most frequently used for capital punishment, the most premeditated form of killing in the world.

Unlimited retaliation, limited retaliation. A third stage might be called limited love. In Leviticus 19:18 it is written: "You shall not take vengeance nor bear a grudge

2. Exodus 21:24.

against the children of your own people, but you shall love your neighbor as yourself."[3]

Again, a step forward. Limited love is better than limited retaliation, and limited love can be very moving—a mother's love for her child, children's love for their parents. But when the neighbor to be loved has been limited to one of one's own people, then limited love, historically, has supported White supremacy, religious bigotry, the Nazi notion of *Herrenvolk*, and "America for Americans" (which never included Native Americans). Actually, limited love is often more self-serving than generous, as Jesus himself recognized when he said, "If you love those who love you, what reward have you? Do not even the tax collectors do the same? And if you only salute your brothers and sisters, what more are you doing than others? Do not even the Gentiles do the same?"[4]

Jesus, of course, was pressing for a fourth state, unlimited love, the love that is of God, the love you give when you make a gift of yourself, no preconditions. (Have you ever noticed how Jesus healed with no strings attached? He didn't say to blind Bartolomeus, now healed, "Now don't you go ogling beautiful women." To the owner of the withered hand he restored Jesus

3. Leviticus 19:18.   4. Matthew 5:46–47.

didn't warn, "No stealing now.") And the neighbor to be loved according to the parable of the Good Samaritan is the nearest person in need regardless of race, religion, or nationality, and we can safely add gender or sexual orientation.

Such was the love that Saint Paul extolled; such was the love of God when at Christmas he gave the world he so loved, not what it deserved but what it needed, his only begotten son that "whosoever should believe in him should not perish but have eternal life."[5]

One of my favorite stories concerns a beggar in sixteenth century Paris who, desperately ill, was taken to the operating table of a group of doctors. In Latin, which they were sure he would not understand, the doctors said, "Faciamus experimentum in anima vile" (Let us experiment on this vile fellow). The beggar, who was actually an impoverished student, later to become a renowned poet, Marc Antoine Muret, replied from the slab on which they had laid him: "Animam vilem appellas pro qua Christus non dedignatus mori est?" (Will you call vile one for whom Christ did not disdain to die?).

If Christ didn't disdain to die for any of us, who are we not to live for all of us?

5. John 3:16.

In order to live for all of us, to strive for the unified advance of the human species, we have to recognize that just as there are two kinds of simplicity—one on the near, the other on the far side of complexity—so there are two kinds of love: one lies on this side of justice, the other on the far side.

Said prophet Amos "Let justice"—not charity—"roll down like mighty waters," and for good reason: whereas charity alleviates the effects of poverty, justice seeks to eliminate the causes of it. Charity is a matter of personal attribute; justice is a matter of public policy.

To picture justice as central, not ancillary, to the Gospel often demands a recasting of a childhood faith. Many of us were brought up to believe that what counts is a personal relationship with God, inner peace, kindness to others, and a home in heaven when all our years have sped.

And many of us never get over the religion of our childhood that we either loved or hated. Either way the results are disastrous.

It is also true that many pastors deliberately perpetuate a childish version of the faith, particularly if they are ministers of mainline middle-class churches, for, not surprisingly, they find it easier to talk to their congregations of charity rather than of justice. Charity, after all, threatens not at all the status quo that may be profitable to a goodly number of their parishioners. Justice, on the other hand, leads directly to political controversy.

So there is a real temptation to think that an issue is less spiritual for being more political, to believe that religion is above politics, that the sanctuary is too sacred a place for the grit and grime of political battle. But if you believe religion is above politics, you are, in actuality, for the status quo—a very political position. And were God the god of the status quo, then the church would have no prophetic role, serving the state mainly as a kind of ambulance service.

In the 1990s, both the Million Man March and the Promise-Keepers let the political order off the hook. Theirs was a purely spiritual message that just happened to parallel the antigovernment message of the Republicans.

By contrast, Martin Luther King Jr. led the 1963 March on Washington and later the Poor People's March to confront the government, to put the government on notice.

The Christian right talks a lot about "traditional values" and "family values." Almost always these values relate to personal rather than social morality. For the Christian right has trouble not only seeing love as the core value of personal life but even more trouble seeing love as the core value of our communal life—the love that lies on the far side of justice. Without question, family responsibility, hard work, compassion, kindness, religious piety—all these individual virtues are of enduring importance. But again, personal morality doesn't threaten the status quo. Furthermore, public good doesn't automatically follow from private virtue. A person's moral character, sterling though it may be, is insufficient to serve the cause of justice, which is to challenge the status quo, to try to make what's legal more moral, to speak truth to power, and to take personal or concerted action against evil, whether in personal or systemic form.

It is no accident that the welfare reform bill is called the Personal Responsibility Act. Most talk of responsibility these days is directed at the most powerless people in our society. If you believe, as do so many members of the Christian right, that the ills of society stem largely from the carelessness and moral failures of America's poor, if you separate economic issues from cultural concerns, if you can't see that economic coercion is "violence in slow motion," that it is the economy that consigns millions to the status of the unwanted, unused, discarded, then you find little need to talk of homelessness, poverty, hunger, inadequate medical care, for these are created by illegitimacy, laziness, drugs, abetted by welfare dependency and sexual deviation. To the Christian right, the American underclass is far more a moral phenomenon than an economic one.

In this fashion the theological individualism of the religious right serves its political and economic conservatism; the victim is blamed for a situation that is largely systemic. What the religious right persists in ignoring is that, although self-help is important, self-help alone will not solve the problems of the poor. And to blame the poor for their oppression and to affirm the affluent in their complacency, to oppose sexual permissiveness and say not a word about the permissiveness of consumerism—which insists that it is right to buy, wrong to defer almost any gratification—these positions are anything but biblical.

Clearly, the love that lies on the far side of justice demands a communal sense of responsibility for and a sense of complicity in the very evils we abhor.

Rabbi Abraham Joshua Heschel, a mentor to so many of my generation, constantly contended that in a free society "some are guilty but all are responsible."

That profound understanding of community has a striking historical example. In the middle of the seventeenth century, Oliver Cromwell sat down to draw up new rules of war for his revolutionary army. He came to the question of what to do with a man found with a wound in his back—someone who fled in the face of the enemy? Cromwell's answer was to round up his friends and drum them out of the army and the church. Why? Because cowardice is a communal failure. More accurately, cowardice is a place where personal and communal responsibilities intersect: "Some are guilty but all are responsible."

If cowardice is a communal failure, so is poverty. It is hardly the fault of those Americans willing, even desperate, to work that there are simply more unskilled workers than unskilled jobs and nowhere near the money necessary for training people to land jobs that would lift them out of poverty. Or consider these two facts: (1) a child of affluent parents is six times more likely to have an undergraduate degree than a child of poor parents; and (2) the odds are 3 to 1 that a pregnant teenager is poor, which suggests that poverty traps girls in pregnancy more than pregnancy traps girls in poverty.

Without question, education is the best way out of dead-end jobs and welfare dependency. Lack of it, then, is another communal failure. A recent study in Washington State showed that 36 percent of those on welfare had learning disabilities that never had been remedied.

Crime is a communal failure. We're not tough on crime, only on criminals. Were we tough on crime, we'd put the money up front, in prevention rather than in punishment. We'd be building healthier communities, not more and more prisons. "Some are guilty but all are responsible." We stress the guilty in order to exonerate the responsible.

In short, it is not enough to be a Good Samaritan, not when, from North Philadelphia to East Oakland, whole communities lie bleeding in the ditch. What the poor need today is not piecemeal charity but wholesale justice.

And that's what is so lacking today. "The comfortable are in control," as John Kenneth Galbraith wrote a short while ago, and largely because, as another observer put it, "We have the best Congress money can buy." Until we Americans get serious about reforming campaign financing, our politicians will increasingly become lapdogs of the rich.

When I was a boy in public school, I was told that there are rich people and poor people—no connection. When I came to New York, I was told that this was the most exciting city in the world, but "we do have problems"—a lot of poor people. When I read the Bible, I find that the poor are never the problem. It's always the rich who are a problem to the poor, as Oscar Romero, the martyred monsignor of El Salvador, recognized so movingly. Never did he call the poor of his country *los pobres*. He called them *los enpobrecidos*, those *made poor.*

Surely, we should also be calling America's poor "the impoverished," especially when we see our Congress reversing the priorities of Mary's Magnificat, filling the rich with good things and sending the poor empty away. Why, the way we are cutting taxes for the wealthy and social programs for the poor, you'd think the greedy were needy and the needy were greedy!

Why should we back the proposed school vouchers when, without an affluence test, such vouchers are but disguised welfare checks for the rich, many of whose children are already in private schools at the expense of the public school system? As far as I can see, parents wouldn't have freedom of choice; school administrators would. Parents would have freedom to apply.

Some people even deny the need for the government to subsidize a daily guaranteed hot meal for every poor child in the country, and today such children are almost one in four. You have to be morally malnourished so to treat any child of God in the richest country in the world.

And finally, as our welfare system increasingly takes the form of block grants to states, it is safe to assume that the states will cut taxes to attract business, reduce support to cities and to the social programs the cities must provide. Cities will be left with problems undiminished and resources shrinking—a sure recipe for disaster. Even Nixon, though anxious to decentralize education, job training, development, and law enforcement, still wanted a sturdy safety net centralized so that benefits would be uniform, not subject to the shifting political winds of fifty states.

Jesus was certainly something more than a prophet but surely nothing less. And that means, once again, that the love that is the core value of our individual life should also be the core value of our life together. Love has a corporate character as well as a personal one. So just as the simplicity we should embrace lies on the far side of complexity, so the love we should embrace lies on the far side of justice, never on the near side. This understanding is crucial today, when, as I said, no longer is it an individual who lies bleeding in the ditch but whole communities in city after city across the land.

We Americans have so much, and we're asking of ourselves so little. What we are downsizing more than anything else are the demands of biblical justice.

Let Christians remember how Jesus was concerned most for those society counted least and put last. Let us all remember what King and Gandhi never forgot—that for its implementation compassion frequently demands confrontation.

I said at the outset that conventional religious wisdom in Jesus' time stressed correct belief and right behavior. Conventional religious wisdom in America does the same today.

To many American evangelists, faith is a goody that they got and others didn't, an extraordinary degree of certainty that most can't achieve. This kind of faith is dangerous, for it can be and often is worn as a merit badge or used as a club to clobber others.

In contrast, Saint Paul sees faith as confidence in the face of *not* knowing. "For we walk by faith, not by sight."[6] Saint Paul's faith is a thankful response to grace, to the outpouring of God's love, that persistently seeks to get everything right in this world, including us. Such a faith is never exclusive, always inclusive and deeply ethical, never moralistic.

Jesus subverted the conventional religious wisdom of his time. I think we have to do the same. The answer to bad evangelism is not no evangelism but good evange-

6. See 2 Corinthians 5:7.

lism; and good evangelism is not proselytizing but witnessing, bearing witness to "the light that shines in the darkness, and the darkness has not overcome it";[7] bearing witness to the love that burns in every heart, deny it or suppress it as we will; and bearing witness to our version of the truth just as the other side witnesses to its version of the truth—for let's face it, truth in its pure essence eludes us all.

And that's where I think a Christian should stand, one whose heart is "a little to ze left".

7. John 1:5.

HOMOPHOBIA:
THE LAST "RESPECTABLE"
PREJUDICE

ē

I WANT TO CONFRONT homophobia for two reasons.
The first is that the "gay agenda" has replaced the
"communist threat" as the battering ram of reactionary
politics. Instead of a commie behind every bush, there's
a gay person sick and sinful.

The second reason is that while the church has generally given at least some support to the oppressed, in the
case of homosexuals the church has led in the oppression.

The better to refute the assertions of contrary-
minded Christians, I want to speak as a Christian
preacher who shares Bishop Tutu's sorrowful conclusion: "The Lord of the Church would not be where his
church is in this matter."

Preachers do best with texts. Mine this evening

comes from the fourth chapter of Luke, when Jesus, quoting Isaiah, says he is come "to proclaim liberty to the captives and recovery of sight to the blind."

Who are the captives, and what is it these days that holds them in bondage?

Many of us have a strong allergic reaction to change—of any kind. And some of us even go so far as to embrace "The Principle of the Dangerous Precedent" put forth by the British academic who said, "Nothing should ever be done for the first time."

The result is an intolerance for nonconforming ideas that runs like a dark streak through human history. In religious history this intolerance becomes particularly vicious when believers divide the world into the godly and the ungodly; for then, hating the ungodly is not a moral lapse but rather an obligation, part of the job description of being a true believer.

Think how, for example, fleeing British persecution, our Puritan forebears sailed to America, only to become equally intolerant of religious ideas other than their own, which they enforced as the official faith of the Massachusetts Bay colony. First they banned that early church dissident, Anne Hutchinson, who, as she exited the church where the trial was held, said words haunting to this day: "Better to be cast out of the church than to deny Christ." (Everything churchly is not Christlike!)

In 1660 these Puritans went further, hanging Mary Dyer, an early Quaker, for insisting, in effect, "Truth is my authority, not some authority my truth."

Three hundred years later, in the 1960s, this same intolerance made many Christians consider Martin Luther King Jr. more an agitator than a reconciler. And to this day most churches refuse to ordain not only gays and lesbians but *all* women. You'd think that if Mary could carry our Lord and Savior in her body a woman could carry his message on her lips! As for the argument, repeated frequently by the pope John Paul, that there were no women among the original twelve disciples—well, there also were no Gentiles.

Why all this intolerance? Because while the unknown is the mind's greatest need, uncertainty is one of the heart's greatest fears. So fearful, in fact, is uncertainty that many insecure people engage in what psychiatrists call "premature closure." They are those who prefer certainty to truth, those in church who put the purity of dogma ahead of the integrity of love. And what a distortion of the Gospel it is to have limited sympathies and unlimited certainties, when the very reverse—to have limited certainties but unlimited sympathies—is not only more tolerant but far more Christian. For

"who has known the mind of God?" And didn't Saint
Paul also insist that if we fail in love we fail in all things
else?

The opposite of love is not hatred but fear. "Perfect
love casts out fear." Nothing scares me like scared people; for while love seeks the truth, fear seeks safety, the
safety so frequently found in dogmatic certainty, in
pitiless intolerance.

So I believe the captives most in need of release, those
today whose closet doors most need to be flung open,
are really less the victims than their oppressors—the
captives of conformity—the racists, the sexists, the het-
erosexists, all who live in dark ignorance because their
fears have blown out the lamp of reason. So groundless
are these fears that fence them in, I am reminded of the
entry for November 1939 in E. B. White's journal, *One
Man's Meat,* which he wrote while living in Maine:

> A friend of mine has an electric fence around a piece of
> his land, and he keeps two cows there. I asked him one day
> how he liked his fence and whether it cost much to operate.
> "Doesn't cost a damn thing," he replied. "As soon as the
> battery ran down I unhooked it and never put it back. That
> strand of fence wire is as dead as a piece of string, but the
> cows don't go within ten feet of it. They learned their les-
> son the first few days."

Apparently this state of affairs is general throughout the United States. Thousands of cows are living in fear of a strand of wire that no longer has the power to confine them. Freedom is theirs for the asking. Rise up, cows! Take your liberty while despots snore. And rise up too, all people in bondage everywhere! The wire is dead, the trick is exhausted. Come on out!

Yes, come on out, fearful people; the pasture is greener where love prevails and discords end and the joys of unity are proved. Come on out, especially you Christians, because "for freedom Christ has set you free."

Here's what many a Christian has learned: It is absolutely right to love and learn from the sixty-six books of the Bible (seventy-one if you're Roman Catholic). But it is wrong to fear their every word, *for everything biblical is not Christlike*. For example: "Now go and smite Amalek . . . do not spare them, but kill both man and woman, infant and suckling, ox and sheep, camel and ass . . . . Thus says the Lord."[1] Besides, we Christians believe in the Word made flesh, not in the Word made words. And for God's sake let's be done with the hypocrisy of claiming "I am a biblical literalist" when everyone is a

1. See 1 Samuel 15:3.

selective literalist, especially those who swear by the anti-homosexual laws in the book of Leviticus and then feast on barbecued ribs and delight in Monday night football, for it is *toevah,* an abomination, not only to eat pork but merely to touch the skin of a dead pig.

Homosexuality was not a big issue for biblical writers. Nowhere in the four Gospels is it even mentioned. In fact, in all of Scripture only seven verses refer to homosexual behavior.

Although all these verses forbid or deplore homosexual behavior, nevertheless, in many discussions of these texts, thinking is woefully slack. Take, for example, the story of Sodom and Gomorrah. As the cities were already under sentence of doom, the destruction of Sodom could hardly have been the result of the attempted gang rape of the angels. The prophet Ezekiel makes this abundantly clear: "Behold this was the guilt of your sister Sodom. She and her daughters had pride, surfeit of food, and prosperous ease, but did not aid the poor and the needy."[2] Likewise, Isaiah and Amos compare the Israelites of their day to Sodom only because "your hands are full of blood," "the spoil of the poor is in your houses."[3] And the prophet Zephaniah proclaims: "Moab shall become like Sodom, and the Am-

2. Ezekial 16:49.   3. Isaiah 59:3; Amos 4:11.

morites like Gomorrah" for they have filled their
houses "with violence and fraud."[4]

How ironic it is that biblical misreading made
"sodomy" a crime, while the truer crime, gluttony, gets
off scot-free!

If we make the Levitical text on homosexual behavior
normative—"A man shall not lie with another man as
with a woman"—what do we do with other prohibi-
tions? I've already mentioned eating pork; what about
wearing garments made of two different materials and
sowing a field with two kinds of seed?

And what about all the normative behavior in Scripture no longer considered so today? No biblical literalist I know of publically advocates slavery or stoning to
death an adulterer; nor do people today believe, as did
the ancient Israelites, that a man could not commit
adultery against his wife—only against another man by
using the other man's wife.

Polygamy too was regularly practiced, and again it's
ironic that Mormon polygamy was outlawed in America despite Constitutional protection of freedom of religion and despite the fact that it was a biblical practice
nowhere explicitly prohibited in the Bible.

Prostitution was considered natural in Old Testa-

4. Zephaniah 2:29.

ment times and celibacy abnormal. Today the Roman
Catholic Church talks of celibacy as a divine calling,
but in the case of gays it legislates celibacy not by calling but by category.

Saint Paul thought all men were straight. He knew
nothing of sexual orientation. He assumed that all homosexual activity was done by heterosexuals. This as-
sumption is true as well of Old Testament writers,
which means that all the biblical passages used to flay
gays and lesbians have really nothing whatsoever to say
about constitutionally gay people in genuinely loving
relationships.

In short, it would appear that everyone reserves the
right to pick and choose among sexual mores in the
Bible. Says Walter Wink, to whose writings I am much
indebted: "There is no Biblical sex ethic . . . . The Bible
knows only a love ethic . . . . This doesn't mean everything goes. It means that everything is to be critiqued by
Jesus' commandment to love."

When everything biblical is not Christlike, we Christians need to develop an interpretive theory of Scripture. I think the love of Jesus is indeed the plumb line by
which everything is to be measured. And while laws
may be more rigid, love is more demanding, for love insists on motivation and goes between, around, and way
beyond all laws.

In no way do I wish to discount the central role of Scripture. The Bible, after all, is the foundational document for all churches the world around. But if you take the Bible seriously, you *can't* take all of it literally. And you don't honor the higher truth you find in the Bible by ignoring truths found elsewhere. Christians should be impressed by the fact that in 1973 the American Psychological Association declared homosexuality per se was no sign of illness. Likewise, they should heed natural scientists who have discovered homosexuality in mammals, birds, and insects. How, as claimed by Jerry Falwell, could homosexuality be the result of the Fall when mammals, birds, and insects were around long before the human species arrived?

Fundamentalists forget that love demands discernment as well as obedience. Here are two biblical verses they never quote: "Why do you not judge for yourselves what is right?" and "Do you not know that we are to judge angels? How much more matters pertaining to this life?"[5]

Finally, let me say that I am sure that no word of God is God's last word.

Let's turn now to my earlier suggestion that the gay agenda has replaced the communist threat as the battering ram of reactionary politics. Why is this so?

5. Jesus speaking in Luke 12:57; Saint Paul speaking in 1 Corinthians 6:3.

Pride is not accidentally but essentially competitive: I can go up only if someone else or some other group of people goes down. It is for that reason that there is so much conscious or unthinking social subordination in life. And some people can't live without enemies; they need them to tell them who they are. Anticommunists for years needed communists and vice versa.

Gays are natural enemies because of the personal revulsion many straights feel about gay sexual behavior. Sex, let's face it, is dynamite, and we should recognize the power of involuntary revulsion just as we do the power of involuntary attraction.

No one is to be blamed for feeling revulsion. How can you help it in a homophobic society? What's essential is to recognize the cultural source of this revulsion and not to act in ways that hurt others.

What I hold against the religious right is its cruelty. It's cruel because it's ignorant; and as its ignorance stems from self-righteousness and complacency, it is an ethical, not an intellectual default.

Of course, it may be that instead of an irrational prejudice, homophobia represents a completely rational fear of sexuality divorced from reproduction, justified by pleasure alone. If true, heterosexuals are caught between longing for more freedom and fear of losing a more orderly and virtuous, if more repressed, world. Were that the case, then straight people opposed to what they perceive as gay promiscuity should be supporting same-sex unions.

In any event, in a Washington cemetery, on the gravestone of a Vietnam veteran, it is written: "When I was in the military, they gave me a medal for killing two men and a discharge for loving one."

Although the academic community is more tolerant than the religious right, it is also more passive, and tolerance and passivity are a lethal combination. It's easy to forget how frequently compassion demands confrontation.

Confrontation is necessary to shake up the complacent, the "good people" who are indeed "good" but within the limits of their inherited prejudices and traditions. Someone has to play Hamlet to their Horatio. "There are more things in heaven and earth, Horatio, than are dreamt of in your philosophy."[6] Someone has to recall to them Jeremiah: "Woe to those who say 'Peace, peace' where there is no peace"; and Jesus too— "I came not to bring peace but a sword."[7] Surely, he was referring to the sword of truth, the only sword that heals the wounds it inflicts.

6. Act 1, scene 5.   7. Jeremiah 6:14; Matthew 10:34.

Now comes the really hard part, the part only gays
and lesbians can play. The feminist movement in Nor-
way has a slogan, "Not to do to them what they did to
us." In other words, if you are gay and people are
screaming at you that you are a moral pervert, can you
so speak and act as to rob their position of any moral
cogency? Gandhi and Martin Luther King have shown
that it is the temper and spirit with which a movement
conducts itself rather than a particular action that
makes the greatest difference. Divested of moral preten-
sions, a prejudiced person becomes as Samson with his
locks shorn. Nonviolence does not mean turning yourself into a doormat so that people can walk all over you.
But it does mean returning evil with good, violence
with nonviolence, hatred with a love that is obliged to
increase upon pain of diminishing.

Because all this he understood so profoundly, the
great agitator of the 1960s won the Nobel Peace Prize,
and most of America now celebrates a national holiday
in his honor. Because they too, in Christlike fashion, re-
turned evil with good, both Anne Hutchinson and
Mary Dyer have statues in their honor in the center of
the very city where the one was banned and the other
hanged.

The good tidings are that we live in a moral universe.

"God is not mocked." The former foreign minister of Israel, Abba Eban, once remarked, "Human beings really do the right thing, but only after exhausting all alternatives." Already there are signs of progress—the movie *Philadelphia*, the sitcom *Ellen*, the 232 United Church of Christ congregations who have declared themselves "open and affirming" to gays, the 150 Methodist churches who have done the same. Some 10 percent of all Unitarian ministers are openly gay.

Other signs of progress are the gradual de-ghettoization and de-urbanization of gays. More gays are living openly in smaller and smaller towns. And gay-straight alliances are forming in high schools supported in Massachusetts by the Governor's Commission on Gay and Lesbian Youth.

Without doubt, such progress as has been made is due primarily to the determination of the gay community. Despite the AIDS epidemic, so poignantly described in the Psalmist's phrase, "the destruction that wastes at noonday," despite "the band playing on," the legal setbacks in Colorado and Maine, the violence against them that goes on all over the country, the gay communities of America have continued the fight, not for "special rights" but for the equal rights long overdue them. And the fight has been hard, for as every libera-

tion movement has learned, those who benefit from injustice are less able to understand its true character than
those who suffer from it.

Just as African Americans have proved that the problem all along was one of white racism; and women, that
the problem all along was one of male chauvinism; so
gays, lesbians, and bisexuals are proving that God's creation is far more pluralistic than the eyes of many
straights have wished to perceive.

So here's to the gay community and to all it's doing
for all of us. And praise the Lord who brings liberty to
the captives of conformity and recovery of sight to the
blindly prejudiced.

THE AUTHORITY OF
THE BIBLE

℃

HENRY DAVID THOREAU said of the New Testament:
"Most people favor it outwardly, defend it with bigotry,
and hardly ever read it."

In support of his last contention, that people "hardly
ever read it," a recent poll revealed that of the one thou-
sand people interviewed, 16 percent believed that the
New Testament included a book by the apostle
Thomas, and 10 percent thought that Joan of Arc was
Noah's wife.

That's pretty funny but sad as well, for billions of
people down the centuries and across the earth have
heard the word and felt the spirit of God emanating
from biblical pages.

Let me speak personally. I read the Bible because the
Bible reads me. I see myself reflected in Adam's excuses,
in Saul's envy of David, in promise-making, promise-

breaking Peter. I see the violence of the world revealed
in the fact that the first recorded murder in the Bible is a
fratricide. And in reading the Bible's poetry, history,
laws, proverbs, its prophets, and the incomparable
words of and about Jesus—in all those writings I find a
God who bruises our egos but mends our hearts, a God
who pleads without ceasing the cause of the oppressed,
a God who not only answers our questions but, equally
importantly, questions our answers.

In other words, for me as for countless others, the
Bible has incomparable authority. It is, after all, the
founding document of every Christian church in the
world.

But authority is not infallibility. If you take the Bible
seriously, you can't take it literally, not all of it. For instance, let's compare the Bible to modern science. The
writers of the Book of Genesis envisaged the earth as a
relatively flat expanse with water both above and below
it. Clearly, theirs is not a modern scientific view. But
clearly too, the writers of Genesis can't be blamed for
not knowing what science has taught their descendants.
We are the ones who can be blamed if we allow their ignorance to excuse our own.

The writers of Genesis say that God created light on
the first day; not until the fourth day did God create the

sun. We now know that the sun makes daylight and its absence the night. While conceding that point, many fundamentalists still cling to creationism as if biblical authors who did not know that the sun makes day should be more knowledgeable about less obvious issues of science.

Religious fundamentalists sacrifice intellect, emotion, and the honesty of both to the safety of their literalist creed. They don't appreciate the importance of religious myths, which are spiritual truths, not historical facts. They are stories that are not literally, only eternally, true. They strike chords with every generation. Thomas Mann once defined a myth as a truth "that is and always will be, no matter how much we try and say it was."

Let's compare a religious myth to the important American myth that "all people are created equal and are endowed by their Creator with certain inalienable rights"—presumably from the very beginning.

Is that a scientific or historical fact? Can it be proved? Isn't it rather a deep intuitive truth about human worth?

It's good to remember that myths are less concerned with the "how" of things than with the "why" of things. Why did the United States come into being? What's its purpose, its meaning? There's a good adage in journalism: once all the facts are in, no one has the truth. Likewise, the philosopher Wittgenstein contended that once all the scientific questions have been answered, the most important questions remain untouched. That is because the most important questions for human beings concern their values. It is the business of science to provide the facts of natural life, not the values of human life. It is the business of science to deliver us from superstition, not to reveal ultimate truth.

The biblical stories of the creation were written by people who were less interested in the *process* of creation, about which they had no scientific knowledge, than in the *purpose* of creation, which I think they understood far better than most of us. They were less interested in what came first than in what is eternally true, not once and then but now and always. The real concern of all creation stories in all religions is the relation of the known universe to the unknowable God. The conclusion of all creation stories is that the unknowable determines the value of everything that flows from it. And the authors of creation stories, scientifically illiterate, used the daring of the poet to imagine what they could not see.

To insist on a literal interpretation of the creation stories in Genesis is to confuse the "how" and the "why" questions, to confuse facts and meaning. (Remember "once all the facts are in no one has the truth.") It is to pit science against religion, misunderstanding the intentions of both, for the focus of science is facts, and the focus of religion is values and meaning. Literalism splits rather than unifies our consciousness. And as we have seen time and again in history, literalism leads to blind belief, which, like nothing else in the world, begets blind unbelief.

A final and, as always, inadequate analogy. A guidebook to Venice, a Baedeker, will provide the exact details of every point of interest in the city. In Turner's painting of Venice, not a single detail is exact, but oh, the mystery, the wonder, the beauty of that city!

Fallible in matters scientific, the Bible is also fallible in matters historical. To cite only two Gospel examples, the "how" of Jesus' birth appears to be of little importance to both Mark and John, while Matthew and Luke give differing accounts. Likewise, the stories of Jesus' baptism vary: two gospels say Jesus was baptized by John the Baptist, but Luke has John already in prison.

Just as biblical writers are not first and foremost scientists, so they are not historians. First and foremost they are believers. And when they write history, it is from a believer's, an insider's point of view. What they write is what Germans call *Heilgeschichte*—salvation history.

To cite another analogy from American history, here is American salvation history, famously stated from an insider's point of view. "Fourscore and seven years ago our fathers brought forth on this continent a new nation, conceived in liberty and dedicated to the proposition that all men are created equal."

An outsider's point of view might recall thirteen colonies who felt the tax burden to be too great, especially without representation, and therefore declared their independence, which they never would have won without the help of Lafayette and thousands of French troops.

Lincoln wants his fellow Americans to be sure that "these dead shall not have died in vain—that this nation, under God, shall have a new birth of freedom—and that government of the people, by the people, for the people, shall not perish from the earth."

What biblical writers want most is to bring God's people closer to God. The Bible, as they say, is "History" (or Hers).

And finally, the Bible cannot even be an infallible source of belief and morality. "Slaves," says Saint Paul, "be obedient to your masters." In their zeal to live biblically, no fundamentalist I know would today champion the cause of slavery.

"Honor the emperor."[1] Does that injunction mean that no Christian should have served under George Washington or in any revolution before or since?

"Wives, accept the authority of your husbands."[2] Surely, that doesn't mean that feminists who don't want to be masochists are un-Christian.

In other words, New Testament writers, reflecting their time, tolerated forms of oppression we now consider intolerable.

So the Bible is not infallible in matters scientific, historical, or even as regards ethical norms of behavior. And what about biblical miracles?

Allow me a final analogy from American history. What if modern scholarship should one day establish that the silver dollar George Washington hurled across the mighty Rappahannock had, in fact, splashed? Would George Washington still remain, as we were taught in grammar school, "first in war, first in peace, first in the hearts of his countrymen"? The answer, of course, is yes, for the story of the silver dollar is an expression of faith, not a basis of faith. It is the kind of story followers of George Washington, committed to

1. See 1 Peter 2:17.   2. See 1 Peter 3:1.

him on other grounds, would love to tell of him around a good campfire.

Likewise, if Jesus never walked on the Sea of Galilee, he is still to Christians their Messiah. For Christ is not God's magic incarnate but God's love incarnate. He was not one to go around, Houdini-like, breaking the laws of physical nature but rather one who, beyond all limits of human nature, loved as none before nor after him has ever loved. In the face of such awesome love even the waves must rise up and the winds bow down, even as at his birth a star stood still and at his death the earth quaked, rending rocks and splitting graves wide open.

All miracles, including biblical miracles, fall into one of two general categories. There are miracles that are a basis of faith and others that are an expression of faith.

In the story of Jesus walking on the water, the true miracle, the one that is a basis of faith and makes the story eternally if not literally true, takes place when despairing Peter cries out "Lord save me," and Jesus does. That's really the central miracle of every Christian life. When sinking in our sense of helplessness, we reach out for a love greater than we ourselves can ever express, when we reach out for a truth deeper than we could ever articulate and for a beauty richer than we ourselves can ever contain, when we too cry out "Lord, save me," Jesus does. Cry out for a thimbleful of help, and you receive an oceanful in return.

But at some point in all this discussion the question inevitably arises, "Who are we to pick and choose what to believe in sacred Scripture?"

Actually, who are we *not* to pick and choose? Are we not children of God who in return for His/Her love wants our own freely given? And isn't freedom a necessary precondition to love? And doesn't love demand the utmost in clearsightedness?

When I was in seminary, Richard Niebuhr taught that the Bible is "an indispensable means seeking its dispensability." In other words, it is a signpost not a hitching post. It points beyond itself, saying, "Pay attention to God, not me."

It is a mistake to look to the Bible to close a discussion; the Bible seeks to open one. God leads with a light rein, giving us our head. Jesus spoke in parables because these stories have a way of shifting responsibility from the narrator to the hearer. Christians have to listen to the world as well as to the Word—to science, to history, to what reason and our own experience tell us. We do not honor the higher truth we find in Christ by ignoring truths found elsewhere.

I believe every Christian has a right to his or her

opinion about the Bible; our only obligation—and it is a big one—is to have an informed opinion.

I want to conclude with a word about "You gotta believe it 'cause it's in the Bible." You can bet your bottom dollar that the person saying that is not referring to the Sermon on the Mount. Rather he has in mind a passage you have no business believing in—one, for instance, supporting homophobia or gender inequality.

No one says, "You gotta believe it 'cause it's in Shakespeare" or Dante or Goethe or Pushkin. Although not as much as the Bible, these writings still have a lot of authority for a lot of people. The difference is they have no *doctrine* of authority.

Why, for Christians, should the Bible alone have a doctrine of authority, especially when such doctrines demand either a literalist approach which is unacceptable or something which waffles hopelessly?

Why does the Bible need a doctrine of authority? To compel our allegiance? To make us believe something our reason, experience and conscience reject? How can anything outwardly command us that has not first inwardly claimed us? Besides, nobody thinks all biblical passages are of equal worth, that each represents an axis on which our whole faith pivots.

I love the Bible. For over forty years I have preached

on biblical texts that compelled my heart, mind, and soul more than all the books of theology I've ever read. And the Bible stimulates my imagination in ways un-matched even by Blake and Shakespeare.

Sharing my experience, as I said at the outset, are bil-lions of people over time and in every corner of the earth. I don't think we need any "you gotta" doctrines. Just as God doesn't need us to prove God's existence, so the Bible doesn't need a doctrine to affirm its authority. The Bible will continue to have authority for Christians because we hear the word and feel the spirit of God em-anating from its pages.

THE DANGERS
OF SELF-RIGHTEOUSNESS

℃

but man, proud man,
Drest in a little brief authority
Most ignorant of what he's most assured,
His glassy essence, like an angry ape,
Plays such fantastic tricks before high heaven
As make the angels weep.[1]

So, IN *Measure for Measure*, Shakespeare describes many a contemporary world leader. Clearly, self-righteousness is the bane of human relations, be they interpersonal or international.

In individual life the classic biblical example of self-righteousness is the Pharisee who prays, "I thank thee, Lord, that I am not as others are."[2] But in diverse ways nations, too, tend to smugness. For years the French were inordinately pleased with their *mission civilizatrice-*,

1. Act, 1, scene 5.   2. Luke 18:11.

often accompanied by the Foreign Legion. The Swiss are proud of their neutrality and not averse to the money it has brought them. The Germans once considered themselves supermen. The Indians and Chinese feel the age their civilizations boast gives them a corner on the world market for wisdom, while the British, well,

> In the beginning, by some mistake
> Men were foreigners all created,
> 'Til heaven conceived a nobler plan
> And there was born an Englishman.[3]

But these days we Americans are the ones who've got it bad. Time and again our pride-swollen faces close up our eyes. As Ezekiel lamented over proud Tyre: "Your heart was proud because of your beauty; you corrupted your wisdom for the sake of your splendor."[4]

On this national holiday[5] a little soul-searching would not be amiss. American self-righteousness actually has a long lineage reaching perhaps as far back as 1630, when, on board the *Arabella* making its way toward what was to become the Massachusetts Bay colony, John Winthrop said, in a now famous sermon, "We shall be as a city set upon a hill."

3. E. B. White, *One Man's Meat,* Harper & Row, 1983   4. Ezekiel 28:17.
5. February 22, 1998.

As moral aspiration for his Puritan hearers, that image from the Sermon on the Mount was beautiful and appropriate. But it was also fraught with dangerous implications. For "we shall be as a city set upon a hill" implied that others would look up to us, so much so that eventually the world might well be populated largely by frustrated potential Americans. That this has been the prevailing view that many Americans have consistently held of the world and of themselves is indicated by the testimony I now want to bring you from five outstanding Americans.

In the middle of the nineteenth century, Herman Melville, arguably our greatest American novelist, wrote—not in *Moby Dick,* which most of you are probably still trying to finish, but in *White Jacket*—"Long enough have we Americans been skeptics as regards ourselves, and doubted whether the political messiah had come. But he has come—in us—if we would but give utterance to his promptings."

Some fifty years later, at the turn of the century, Albert J. Beveridge informed his senatorial colleagues: "God has marked the United States to lead in the redemption of the world. This is the divine mission of America."

During the war in Vietnam, when tossing his hat into

the presidential ring, Robert Kennedy declared: "At stake is not only the leadership of a party or of a country; at stake is our claim to the moral leadership of the world." Aides begged him to leave the sentence out, the kind that led us into the war in the first place. But their pleadings were in vain.

In 1984, in the course of his second inaugural address, President Reagan said "Peace is our highest aspiration. And our record is clear. Americans resort to force only when they must. We have never been aggressors."

The last sentence would certainly come as news to Native Americans, African Americans, Nicaraguans (where our marines have landed fourteen times), Filipinos, and Cubans, not to mention Vietnamese and Cambodians, and, I daresay, to Teddy Roosevelt had he been tuned in to President Reagan's second inaugural.

And finally, on the *Today Show*, Madeleine Albright recently declared: "If we have to use force, it is because we are America. We are the indispensable nation. We stand tall. We see further into the future."

Listening to her, I was reminded of the Frenchman who said, "Ma patrie, se lève; je la préféré assise" (My country is getting up; I prefer it seated).

The testimony of these five outstanding Americans reminds us on Washington's birthday that the best patriots are not uncritical lovers of their country, any more than they are the loveless critics of it. True patriots carry on a lover's quarrel with their country, a reflection of God's eternal lover's quarrel with the entire world.

No nation is well served by delusions of its righteousness. Every nation makes decisions based on self-interest and then defends them in the name of morality. St. Augustine warned: "Never fight evil as if it were something that arose totally outside of yourself." He was reflecting Saint Paul's contention that "all have sinned and fallen short." The temptation, of course, is to say, "Some have sinned"—that "evil empire" as Reagan called the Soviet Union or that "rogue state" as we call Iraq and five other countries. But Saint Paul insists that *all* have sinned, which says, most importantly, that if nations are not one in love at least we are one in sin, which is no mean bond, because it precludes the possibility of separation through judgment. That is the meaning of the biblical injunction "Judge not, that ye be not judged."[6]

Today, on Washington's birthday, let us also recall that our Declaration of Independence calls for "a decent respect to the opinions of mankind," something

6. Matthew 7:1.

we're not showing when, alone with Israel, we maintain sanctions against Cuba or whenever we preempt and undermine the authority of the United Nations.

The ancient Roman Tacitus defined patriotism as entering into praiseworthy competition with our ancestors. Why not compete with Moses and Joshua, with Washington and Jefferson? As they declared their independence—the first two from Egypt, the second two from England—let us declare our *inter*dependence with all people. On this national holiday let us dare to see pragmatically that the survival unit in our time is no longer an individual nation or an individual anything. The survival unit in our time and henceforth is the whole human race and its environment.

The United States doesn't have to lead the world; it has first to join it. Then, with greater humility, it can play a wiser leadership role.

I said at the outset that self-righteousness was the bane of human relations. I hope you agree with me that individuals and nations are at their worst when, persuaded of their superior virtue, they crusade against the vices of others. They are at their best when they claim their God-given kinship with all humanity, offering prayers of thanks that there is more mercy in God than sin in us.

THE WARHORSE

❦

THE DREAM OF a warless world is hoary with antiquity. And the inexpressible sadness of every era is that each time the dream revives, it dies, overcome by the harshness of reality.

Peace seems always a weary way off. The end of the cold war produced a stillborn dove with unflexed wings. The Pentagon continues to spend some $500,000 a minute, $8,000 a second, on a military budget four times that of Russia, and seventeen times the combined military budgets of the so-called rogue nations—Libya, Syria, Iraq, Iran, North Korea, and Cuba.

How many things we Americans are paying for that we don't need, and how many things we need that we are not willing to pay for!

In matters of war and peace the Bible is ambiguous. Age after age, peacemakers have repeated the grand words inscribed on the Isaiah Wall opposite the United

Nations. "And they shall beat their swords into ploughshares, their spears into pruning hooks; nation shall not lift up sword against nation, neither shall they learn war anymore."[1]

Yet the third chapter of Joel proclaims a time to "beat ploughshares into swords, pruning hooks into spears; let the weak say, 'I am a warrior.'"[2]

The church has been no less ambivalent. Is pacifism true obedience to the Gospel or a false idealism based on the sentimentalization of radical evil?

Actually, everybody is ambivalent. Albert Camus talked of going forward "with weapons in our hands and a lump in our throats."

About the use of force I think we *should* be ambivalent—the dilemmas are real. All we can say for sure is that while force may be necessary, what is wrong—always wrong—is the desire to use it.

For all the Bible's ambivalence there always emerges, in moments of crisis, a prophetic word that insists on being heard and heeded. Often this word subverts musty conventional wisdom, saying in effect, "Forget your self-deceiving rhetoric. The solution you propose has no power to cure." Such a word today is verse 17 of

1. Isaiah 2:4.   2. Joel 3:10.

Psalm 33: "The warhorse is a vain hope for victory, and by its great might it cannot save."

I'm wary—believe me, I'm wary—of ineffectual purity, but I am also convinced that unless we take this verse to our hearts, unless and until war is buried in history along with slavery, colonialism, and apartheid, the human race is likely to go the way of the dinosaur, which became extinct through too much armor and too little brain.

Who can doubt the warhorse's contemporary might? Only God has the authority to end all life on earth, but we have the power, the technical means to destroy the whole of civilization in a single act. The cold war is over, but there are still some 20,000 nuclear weapons around, 95 percent of them American and Russian. That's the equivalent of 750,000 Hiroshima-size bombs or 1.7 tons of TNT for every person on earth. Successive U.S. governments have made it national policy to eliminate chemical and biological weapons, these weapons being relatively cheap and easy to produce and therefore weapons of choice of terrorists and Third World countries. But with most Americans in accord, our political leaders have tenaciously clung to *our* weapon of choice—nuclear weapons.

E. L. Doctorow wrote:

> The bomb first was our weapon,
> Then it became our diplomacy,
> Next it became our economy,
> Now it's become our culture.
> We've become the people of the bomb.

But the great might of the warhorse is "a vain hope for victory," for what we and other nuclear powers are practicing is really nuclear apartheid. A handful of nations have arrogated to themselves the right to build, deploy, and threaten to use nuclear weapons while policing the rest of the world against their production. The nuclear bomb tests recently carried out by India and Pakistan were as predictable as they were terrible because nuclear apartheid has no more chance of succeeding than did racial apartheid in South Africa.

Nuclear apartheid is a recipe for proliferation, a policy of disaster foreseen by the late Rajiv Gandhi, who underscored the moral contradiction of such a policy. "History," he said in a 1988 speech at the United Nations, "is full of myths parading as iron laws of science: that men are superior to women; that the white race is superior to colored races; that colonization was a civilizing mission;

and that nations that have nuclear weapons are responsible powers while those that do not, are not."

How can we Americans claim to be a responsible power when we profess humane ideals and threaten unlimited slaughter? How could the then Soviet Union claim to be a responsible power when they and we together, for forty-odd years, in the sacred name of deterrence, engaged in a nuclear arms race so open-ended that the world became like a prisoner in a cell, condemned to death, awaiting the uncertain moment of execution?

President Clinton was, of course, right to say, "Nuclear weapons are not a manifestation of greatness." But why did he address those words to India and Pakistan alone when the other nuclear powers are hopelessly in love with their pitiless weapons?

How long are we going to burden God's patience with our pious professions!

Fortunately, there is a nascent movement, Abolition 2000, an ever growing number of citizens worldwide who are convinced that early on in the nuclear era Einstein was right. "It is appallingly clear that our technology has surpassed our humanity." These citizens are certain that nuclear weapons threaten far more than they deter catastrophic conflict. They are aware of the nuclear material and know-how that slips quietly across national borders into hands whose owners await eagerly and imminently their nuclear arsenals. Abolition 2000 includes sixty-three generals and admirals from seventeen countries, among them General George Lee Butler, former SAC commmander, a man for thirty-seven years steeped in nuclear weapons and nuclear targets, and General Goodpaster, former supreme commander of NATO forces in Europe.

All of these outstanding citizens want to see, under the most stringent possible international control, not the reduction of nuclear weapons everywhere (because even a small number suggests that the unthinkable is still thinkable); they want all nuclear weapons abolished. The danger of cheating can be countered, they insist, by weapons far more "target-specific" than nuclear weapons.

What will the churches do?

Christians worship a God of truth, which means that discernment is altogether as important as obedience. Love demands the utmost in clearsightedness. Thus, Christians should have much to say to nations whose pride-swollen faces have closed up their eyes, whose power has driven intelligence underground—nations that like proud Tyre, in Ezekiel's words, "have corrupted their wisdom for the sake of their splendor."

And there shouldn't be a Christian born who wouldn't say amen to the words of Monsignor Bruce Kent: "We did not make the planet; we do not own the planet; and we have no right to wreck the planet."

Christians should stand above the nation's nightscape like the illuminated spires of their churches. Every spire symbolizes "a longing for the transcendence of the heavens toward which it draws the eye; but also for the completion of work on the earth in which it is firmly rooted."[3]

Our task is to save the earth, the earth that, as Scriptures tells us, "is the Lord's and the fullness thereof, the world and they that dwell therein."[4]

And for guidance in this task let us not look overly to our political leaders. Their ethical impulses tend to be so much weaker than their political ones that in order not to stand out they'll do almost anything to fit in. They're right to think that politics is the art of the possible but wrong to forget that politics is also the art of making possible tomorrow what seems impossible today.

Once again it is up to us, to those furthest from the seats of power and thereby nearer to the heart of things. So let us not wear an air of futility like a crown of thorns. Let us not hesitate to lead. Only after we have

3. James Carrol, Boston *Globe*, 15 October 1996.   4. Psalm 24:1.

proposed, educated, advocated, lobbied will our politicians consent. The people's movement to ban the land mines had it right: "Together," as Jody Williams said when accepting the Nobel Peace Prize, "we are a super power. It's a new definition of super power. It's not one of us, it's all of us."

If citizens in the nuclear weapons states work together, as they did to ban the land mines, the members of Abolition 2000 think it conceivable that in the year 2000 the nuclear powers might finally answer the request made two years ago by the overwhelming majority of the General Assembly of the United Nations, namely, to call a conference that would set a time-bound framework within which, if not war, at least all nuclear weapons would be buried in history along with slavery, colonialism, and apartheid.

Almost forty years ago I went to visit Kurt Hahn, the founder of Outward Bound. He said to me, "Reverend Coffin, you are looking at an old man in a hurry." Now I know how he felt. I don't expect to see fulfilled the ancient dream of a warless world, not in the short time left to me. But before I die, I want to see all nuclear missiles beaten into homes for the homeless and land for the landless, into day-care centers and good schools for our poorest kids and compassionate care for our elderly.

Nuclear apartheid is utopian and arrogant. Therefore, the abolition of nuclear weapons is a matter of conscience and of profound self-interest. God is not mocked: what is grossly immoral cannot in the long run be politically expedient. With every passing hour it becomes clearer: "The warhorse is a vain hope for victory, and by its great might it cannot save."

CIVILITY, DEMOCRACY,
AND MULTICULTURALISM

C

THERE ARE A NUMBER of books these days on the subject of civility, written for the most part by those who grieve the demise of civil discourse. Personally, I worry more about what's happening to civil rights than to civil discourse, and I certainly wouldn't want to talk about civility if all it meant was good manners, manners often at the expense of morality.

But if we define civility as a profound ethic, practically synonymous with morality, as does Stephen Carter in his book entitled *Civility*, then we can see that without a healthy dose of it our presently ailing democracy has small chance of recovering.

Let me start with a few words about diversity. Clearly, God is more comfortable with diversity than we are. After all, She made it! We, on the other hand, tend to fear our differences more than we celebrate them. In fact, diversity may be the hardest thing for a society to live with and perhaps the most dangerous thing for a society to be without.

While often alarming, it should come as no surprise that people everywhere are today very much alive to their own nationality, ethnicity, race, gender, sexual orientation—all those legitimate differences within our common humanity. For the universalism that is their opposite has too often blurred and denied, not to say vigorously repressed, them. So all over the world, people are asserting the particular over and against the universal. It's something we simply have to accept, for people cannot be asked to serve a greater whole until they have been acknowledged as individually significant.

The challenge, then, is to recognize that the world is about two things: differentiation and communion. The challenge is to seek a unity that celebrates diversity, to unite the particular with the universal, to recognize the need for roots while insisting that the point of roots is to put forth branches. What is intolerable is for differences to become idolatrous. No human being's identity is exhausted by his or her gender, race, ethnic origin, national loyalty, or sexual orientation. All human beings have more in common than they have in conflict, and it is precisely when what they have in conflict seems overriding that what they have in common needs most to be affirmed. James Baldwin described us well: "Each of us, helplessly and forever, contains the other—male in female, female in male, white in black and black in white. We are part of each other."

I hope those few comments suffice to make clear that if civil discourse in America is declining, it is not because at some earlier time our values were superior. Some may have been; many weren't. But one thing they were—those values were more pervasive: traditions were less questioned; experience was more predictable. Fifty years ago in our public schools, boys took wood shop, girls, home economics. At that time feminists were all but unheard of, homosexuals were closeted, and no one knew any Muslims. Racial segregation was accepted; it was the way America had always done business. There was a single American religion, a highly nationalistic form of Protestant Christianity. There was one enemy—the Soviet Union. And as recently as the early 1960s, as Stephen Carter points out, there was really only one baseball team—the Yankees (recently resurrected); only one basketball team—the Celtics; one football team—the Green Bay Packers; and hockey was dominated by the Montreal Canadians.

Then in the fall of 1964 an aging and White Yankee

team lost the World Series to the St. Louis Cardinals led by its four Black stars—Bob Gibson, Bill White, Lou Brock, and Curt Flood. Racial privileges were now under attack, fortunately by forces for the most part committed to nonviolence. Feminists also began to mount a successful assault against gender inequality. (Today there are no tomboys, only women athletes. There was apparently very little gender discrimination in this month's national elections.) Gays and lesbians began to demand not "special" rights as is often asserted but equal rights. So by the time the Vietnam War had torn the country yet further apart, there were multiple meanings to being an American, and ever since then we have had less and less of a shared understanding of what American democracy is fundamentally about. Clearly, our political battles today prompt more anger than dialogue.

We do well to try to understand those who feel dispossessed by change, who feel they have lost control and power. Said one aging male WASP, "I don't care what the liberation movement—women's liberation, black, Chicano, gay liberation—I always come out Pharoah." Pathetic but understandable.

Clearly the Christian right is a tribe that feels slighted. I think we should oppose its views—vigorously. But I also think we should understand the fears that prompt the views. Of course, it's often difficult to argue with members of the Christian right because what is emotionally rooted is not intellectually soluble!

I said that diversity may be the hardest thing for a society to live with. J. Anthony Lucas concluded *Common Ground*, his moving book on the integration of the public schools in Boston, with the sad suggestion that you can have diversity *or* community, one or the other but not both. I hope he's wrong, but in any event to affirm both differentiation and communion is, I believe, the real challenge of civility.

But before turning to civility, let's recognize how the demands of diversity have also threatened the stability of academic communities, which are generally averse to change. ("How many tenured professors does it take to change a light bulb?" "Change?!")

To their credit, admissions people have become far more intentional in recruiting minorities. You *have* to seek out people to whom life appears a game that often is rigged against them. This special recruitment is beneficial to everyone because our lives are rife with misconceptions of each other *and of ourselves*. Universities should be communities to rescue us from bias and self-deception, and the two are interrelated; to quote James

Baldwin again, "If I am not what you say I am, then you are not who you think you are."

As multiculturalism includes Third World cultures, it is encouraging that professors of French literature now often assign novels by Algerians, Senegalese, and Vietnamese. Likewise, professors of Spanish literature include the poetry of Pablo Neruda and other works by Latin Americans, while the Nigerian Nobel Prize winner Wole Soyinka and other Africans are frequently read in courses on English literature.

But clearly lacking are sufficient minority and women faculty, also minority and women university administrators. And rarely does the canon of American education include the challenging histories of race, class, and sexual orientation.

Let me now turn to civility, which, as I said at the outset, has only superficially to do with manners, etiquette, or even good taste. Taste and truth can sometimes be in serious civil conflict. I remember how, at the height of the war in Vietnam, when half a million Americans there were commanded by General Westmoreland, our country was subjected to one of those periodic crusades by citizens who want to rid public libraries of what they deem to be "dirty books." It was at that point that Norman Mailer arose to say to these little inquisitors of Puritan America: "All the dirty words in all the dirty books you want banned from our public libraries are not to be compared with one minute in the mind of General Westmoreland."

At its most profound, civility has little to do with taste, everything to do with truth. And the truth it affirms, in religious terms, is that everyone, from the pope to the loneliest wino on the planet, is a child of God, equal in dignity, deserving of equal respect. It is a religious truth that we all belong one to another; that's the way God made us. From a Christian point of view, Christ died to keep us that way, which means that our sin is only and always that we put assunder what God has joined together.

Such a belief obviously celebrates rather than fears our human differences. Such a belief affirms both differentiation and community.

Actually, the Declaration of Independence says much the same thing: "We hold these truths to be self-evident, that all men are created equal, that they are endowed by their Creator with certain unalienable rights."

Let me suggest that for over two hundred years the great social struggles of America have aimed to make the Constitution more consonant with the Declaration of Independence. Counting the first ten, the Bill of

Rights, the Constitution now has twenty-six amendments. The eleventh, passed in 1795, is about federal judicial jurisdiction; two are about Prohibition and its repeal; three others deal with the presidency—election, limitation, succession. The other twenty—every one, whether it be granting freedom to slaves or votes to women, outlawing the poll tax or instituting the income tax, lowering the voting age or giving residents of D.C. the right to vote for the president—every one mandates an extension of democracy.

I believe one significant cure for what presently ails us lies in extending yet further our democracy. We need more women's rights, not less, until they are genuinely equal to men's rights. We need more gay rights, more rights for immigrants, for children, for the more than one million of our citizens in jail. We need to recognize that affirmative action is good for all of us as the ex-presidents of Harvard and Princeton have recently reported. And given the vast wealth and power that have accumulated in the hands of a small and self-serving corporate elite, which pays itself proportionately more and pays workers proportionately less than in any other industrialized democracy, we need to democratize the market economy of America. I can still remember from high school days—it was in 1939—hearing Franklin

Roosevelt say, "My fellow Americans, progress is not measured by how much we add to the abundance of those who already have a great deal, but rather by how much we do for those who have too little."

Those who live in safety have a hard time understanding lives steeped in misery, and education these days is of little help. In fact, the greatest damage to both American democracy and to the planet everywhere is done not by the poor and ignorant, for whom education is the solution, but by those who hold B.A.s, B.S.s, L.L.D.s, M.B.A.s, and Ph.Ds, for whom self-interest is the problem. In our country the freedom properly enjoyed by university faculty and students alike, to think and say pretty much what they want—that freedom today is vastly exalted over any obligation to do any good to anyone.

Something has happened to our understanding of freedom. Centuries ago Saint Augustine called freedom of choice the "small freedom," *libertas minor*. *Libertas maior*, the big freedom, was to make the right choices, to be fearless and selfless enough to choose to serve the common good rather than to seek personal gain.

That understanding of freedom was not foreign to our eighteenth-century forebears who were enormously influenced by Montesquieu, the French thinker who differentiated despotism, monarchy, and democracy. In each he found a special principle governing social life. For despotism that principle was fear; for monarchy, honor; and for democracy, not freedom but virtue. In *The Broken Covenant,* Robert Bellah quotes him as writing that "it is this quality, rather than fear or ambition, that makes things work in a democracy."

According to Bellah, Samuel Adams agreed: "We may look to armies for our defense, but virtue is our best security. It is not possible that any state should long remain free where virtue is not supremely honored."

Freedom, virtue—these two were practically synonymous in the minds of our revolutionary forebears. To them it was inconceivable that an individual would be granted freedom merely for the satisfaction of instincts and whims. Freedom was not the freedom to do as you please but rather, if you will, the freedom to please to do as you ought! Freedom, virtue—they were practically synonymous a hundred years later in the mind of Abraham Lincoln when, in his second inaugural address, he called for "a new birth of freedom." But today, because we have so cruelly separated freedom from virtue, because we define freedom in a morally inferior way, our country is stalled in what Herman Melville

called the "Dark Ages of Democracy," a time when, as
he predicted, the New Jerusalem would turn into Baby-
lon, and Americans would feel "the arrest of hope's advance."

For this sorry state of affairs the religious communities of America bear a large measure of the blame. Allow
me to make a rather extended point in this regard.
When it comes to virtue, the leaders of the Christian
right can't seem to distinguish between violations of
personal morality and the great moral issues facing our
society as a whole. They call for the removal of our way-
ward President Clinton even though they must know,
Bible readers that they are, that the Lord did not depose
King David after his shameless seduction of Bathsheba,
nor even after he masterminded the murder of her hus-
band Uriah. But toward the end of his life, David was
not allowed to build the Temple because, as he ex-
plained to his son Solomon, "the word of the Lord
came to me saying, 'You shall not build a house to my
name because you have shed so much blood before me
on earth.' "[1]

There is more than a suggestion here that the Christian right and the rest of us should have been angrier at
President Clinton for his bombing in the Sudan and

1. See 1 Chronicles 22:28.

Afghanistan. Certain it is that we would have had fits if the British, in retaliation for the IRA bombings of London, had bombed Dublin. And maybe we should be angry too at his continued insistence on the kind of sanctions in Iraq that, far from toppling the hated dictator, represent a form of institutionalized child abuse. (If there are "smart" sanctions, there are also dumb ones.)

Virtue in mainline churches may be better focused, but moral outrage is feeble. Most Protestant churches are down to management and therapy.

And in the academic world, too, there's little passion for social justice. It's my experience that students may be repelled by materialism, but they are caught up in it. They may be troubled by persistent poverty, but they overly esteem wealth. And teaching plays a large part in all this. Perhaps for too long in the humanities we've given primacy to concepts, to objective analysis, so that the truth *before us* somehow doesn't get *in us*. For example, we all give intellectual assent to the notion that all people are created equal, but how many of us feel the monstrosity of inequality? That's qualitatively another kind of knowledge.

But that's a big subject for another day and one better addressed by others.

My hope today is that we can agree on this: we should not be graduating students to serve the system;

we should be graduating students to run the system and to run it so that American democracy doesn't become a government of, by, and for the relative few. Were our government for the *people* , we would have the best education in the world, universal health insurance, a decent way of financing elections, and a massive commitment to sources of clean energy.

In his dying breath, Baron von Hugel, a great Christian layman, said, "Caring is the greatest thing, caring matters most." He understood that in old age death is no great tragedy. What is tragic are all the little deaths that precede it, breeding ever greater indifference, the true enemy of the good.

Caring, I believe, is what civility, profoundly understood, is all about. If we recover an understanding of *libertas maior*, if we reunite freedom and virtue by caring ceaselessly for one another, for our multicultural communities, nation, and planet, affirming both differentiation and communion, then our democracy, presently stalled, will once again feel the advance of hope. If we Americans aspire to become a more caring people, democracy and multiculturalism will more than survive; they will thrive. In this century we Americans have created a world for some of us; it's time, in the next century, to create one for all of us.

UNIVERSITY PRESS OF NEW ENGLAND publishes books under its own imprint and is the publisher for Brandeis University Press, Dartmouth College, Middlebury College Press, University of New Hampshire, Tufts University, and Wesleyan University Press.

LIBRARY OF CONGRESS CATALOGING-IN-PUBLICATION DATA
Coffin, William Sloane.
The heart is a little to the left : essays on public morality / by William Sloane Coffin.
    p.   cm.
ISBN 0–87451–958–6 (cloth :   alk. paper)
1. Social ethics   2. Social values.   3. Moral conditions.
I. Title.
HM665.C64   1999
303.3`72—dc21   99–34297